Twists and Turns

A Handbook On Life and Living
FOR ANYONE 12 AND OLDER

Written by
Lori Gayle Bailey

authorHOUSE®

AuthorHouse™
1663 Liberty Drive, Suite 200
Bloomington, IN 47403
www.authorhouse.com
Phone: 1-800-839-8640

First published by AuthorHouse   5/11/2009

ISBN: 978-1-4389-5468-4 (sc)

Library of Congress Control Number: 2009902248

Printed in the United States of America
Bloomington, Indiana

This book is printed on acid-free paper.

Table of Contents

Foreword

Many people would ask who I am and why I think I should write a book.

I am not a famous celebrity or a person whose name most people would recognize. I am, however, a person who has gathered a collection of life experiences that is far broader than the average person's, and I really want to share some of the insights into the way things *really are* with others. How young or old I am is irrelevant. What is relevant is what I have learned, and that knowledge is why I am writing this book.

I couldn't have written this book without the help of many. Those whose names follow have influenced me throughout my life and may recognize themselves in the pages that follow. If that happens, I will have presented your story accurately and that is my goal. Those I am grateful to have not necessarily been involved directly with the writing of this book, but have been a presence in my life at one point or another, and have given me experiences that have led me to the creation of this book.

First and foremost, I must thank my mother and father, for without them I would not have had life and thus could not have written anything. More than that, they gave me a secure family life and an innate sense of values that have shaped the pages of this book in many ways.

I also wish to express never ending gratitude to Gail, Missy, Shirley and Rayford, Randy, Uncle Cecil, Robert, Ginger and Darin, Tina and Wayne, all the wonderful women who preceded me in my family tree, Maw, Ebby, my neighbors and friends in Arlington, and all the parents of Rosanne's past soccer teammates. I also can't forget George Taplin, Ashley Alfaro, Allison Randolph, and all the many wonderful professors I have had for my college classes in recent years. Ralph, Pat, Randy W., Helen, William, Rebecca, Billie, Keith, Tina, Kathy and Charles, Ms. Wright, Rusty, Russell, and Betty, and the list goes on and on.

My greatest gratitude has to go to my beautiful granddaughter Rosanne, who I have been blessed with since the day she was born. Never have I seen such beauty in a human being or as much potential for greatness in years to come. Thank you for learning from me and also for teaching me so much more than you could ever know. Forgive my shortcomings, and know that my love is boundless and unconditional for you. You are the best gift this life on earth will ever see me receive.

I also have to thank, though ironic as it seems, GWP, HNP, and FMB. Though each in their own way nearly ruined my life and/or tried to take it from me, they didn't succeed and they never will. Their horrors imposed upon me have only served to make me smarter and stronger, and for that I must thank them.

And finally I must thank a very special lady, Dr. M. She is the one who told me to "write that book." I was in the process of writing it, but her words confirmed to me the need for this information to be made available in written form.

This book is religiously neutral and politically correct. That part was easy. Truths of the nature presented in the pages that follow transcend all barriers of religion and politics and stand alone. They are just true.

There is humor to be found in every situation as well as something that can be learned.

Life is supposed to be fun.

Introduction

Like a maze, life consists of many twists and turns, and even dead ends. In the same manner you would use a GPS system to find your way to someplace you have never been before, you can use this book to help you navigate life's twists and turns. It was written to show the "real deal" about a number of things.

This book is intended for, and hopefully will be read first and foremost by, those who are in junior high or high school and looking ahead to college in a few years. However, the wisdom imparted in the pages that follow can be read and embedded into the minds and hearts of persons of all ages.

I don't claim to be an expert, but I speak from personal experience and know this book contains truths that can be held up to the light and found to be true, at least when the words were committed to paper.

Some of the things in this book will possibly change, in the light of societal changes and the passage of new laws, and over that I have no control.

However, the majority of what you will read in the pages that follow involves conceptual truths that can't and won't change unless humans change in some drastic way, and those types of evolutionary changes are only exacted over many thousands, possibly millions, of years.

Please know that the purpose of this book is to enlighten and to teach. The things I impart to my readers are not always things that you might want to hear, but have been proven through the passage of years and things I wish I had been exposed to at the age of my intended audience. Knowing some of these things would have made a great difference in the course of my life, and it is my hope that by sharing these things with you that your life in some way may be better and easier to understand after you read this.

If my tone at times sounds cynical, that is not my intent. However, some things in life when explained can only sound cynical in their truth and the irony contained within that truth.

Enjoy this book, and read it more than once. Carry it with you as a reference guide if you so desire.

I want you to know that your life can be whatever you want it to be, but there are some things that just are the way they are and you have to deal with that and continue on towards your dreams. Most adults and senior citizens would not say that their lives had been easy. Easy isn't what it's all about, because as humans we rise to action when we are challenged. Only through extreme conditions have some of the most innovative and wonderful inventions come about.

Many failures precede actual accomplishments, and your life won't prove to be any different in varying degrees. In fact, your life up to this point contains quite a few examples of this already. You learned to walk, didn't you? But only after hundreds of falls on your rear end first. The same goes for riding a bike, skating, and the list goes on.

> **Remember that you only fail when you actually quit trying.**
> **Whether you think you can or think you can't, you are right.**

Remember again that life can be whatever it is you want it to be, but you must realize you will encounter detours, potholes in the road, and may have to endure having the rug pulled out from under you with no warning. That's okay. You just have to get up, dust yourself off, and know that you can overcome just about anything if you believe in yourself. Doubts and fears creep in at times no matter how positive your outlook, but when you learn to quickly replace them with ideas of expected success, you will be able to achieve that success and live your dreams.

Realize that this book was written to offer a bit of insight into many ideas and actual life events. There may prove to be some contradictions between something you have been taught in a classroom and something you read here. This book's purpose is to enlighten you to *reality* as opposed to theory and/or common belief. Theoretical interpretations can and do vary greatly from real life experiences. Many of the concepts circulating in life are embraced from the "ideal" point of view, but sadly ideal situations rarely if ever exist.

Ask questions. Bring it up for classroom or home discussion. Discover the reality as opposed to the theory for yourself somehow. By so doing, you have challenged your mind to learn something new and something that will serve you well throughout your lifetime.

I have always known that after graduation from either high school or college, when a person enters the real world and starts a life on their own, they are ill-prepared for many things. Thus was born the idea for this book. Education comes from many places besides the actual classroom, and life has become so much more complicated than it was even a decade ago. Therefore, I offer this book as a "life primer" to round out the classroom studies and help you with the little nuances that no one ever seems to explain to you but you must know in order to survive. In order to "make it through."

This book is written in the same manner that I speak. I have always been able to hold the attention of those I am addressing in conversation, and therefore I decided to write the book as if I were giving a series of lectures. (To those educators and English professionals who read this, I willingly accept the fact that this is not at all times written in "acceptable" composition form, and for that I apologize. However, I truly believe the message will be better understood in the form it is presented in the pages that follow.)

Reading this book is all I expect of most of you at this point.
Remembering something I said in this book is a step in the right direction.
Realizing the truth contained in these pages is my true purpose.

Enjoy the journey through the pages that follow.

Chapter I.

Fair

What you do think of when you hear the word "fair"? Really think about this for a few minutes before you read any further.

The Merriam-Webster dictionary defines the adjective "fair" as "marked by impartiality and honesty: free from self-interest, prejudice, or favoritism: free from favor toward either or any side."

The same word as a noun is defined as "a competitive exhibition usually with accompanying entertainment and amusements: an exhibition designed to acquaint prospective buyers or the general public with a product: an exposition that promotes the availability of services or opportunities."

As a child and possibly even until the day you read this, you at some time have complained, most likely to a parent, that something in life wasn't fair. "That's not fair!"

I am 100% sure that statement was true at the time you said it in the particular situation. It has been said by probably every child at some time in life and may still be spouted out of your mouth even today.

You must accept and know that life *is not fair, nor will it ever be.* As soon as you realize to the depths of your being that this is true, it makes everything easier.

When you expect circumstances to be fair, you just set yourself up for one disappointment after another, leaving you frustrated, unhappy, and many times despondent. This can lead to depression, health problems, and even criminal activity as a way to "get back at life" for treating you unfairly.

Trust me; these will not change the fact that *life is not fair. It wasn't intended to be and it never will be. We must accept things as they are, and not assume or expect it to be fair. Not from our viewpoint, nor from that of anyone else.*

There will always be those in this life that have less than you do, and there will always be those in this life that have more than you do. I'm not necessarily speaking of material possessions, though that is one of the first ways we as children start to notice and feel that life isn't fair. I'm also speaking of things like opportunity, work, treatment by other people, and even this country's justice system. I will now expand on these for you in order to give you some very real life examples in order to prove what I have just told you.

As a child growing up, you became aware that some of your friends and classmates drove better cars, had more expensive clothes, and lived in bigger houses than you. In today's world, many children are being raised by only one parent. Many are being raised by grandparents in the absence of one or both parents. These types of things become obvious to a child at a young age.

Some child you knew took dance lessons, played the violin, and was enrolled in cheerleading. Another child played football, baseball, and played in the school band.

Then there was the child that never was involved in any type of extracurricular activities, and who went home each day after school and did nothing but homework, chores and watching TV. Their weekends were nothing but staying home and playing or watching TV.

We don't know the reason behind any of the examples above. It could be the parents pushing the child to dance, play an instrument, or try to become a famous athlete. The child might actually exhibit greater-than-normal talent in these areas and really want to pursue these things. The parents could be so deathly afraid that their child will veer off into the world of drugs, gangs, etc. that they have vowed to never give them a spare moment to consider these options. The stay-at-home child could be unable to afford these activities, or could have parents that are so involved in their work that they can't devote the time and/or money to allow their child's participation in extracurricular activities.

However, what I know you were thinking while reading the above was that in some way "that isn't fair" to the child that is never involved in activities of any kind. And from the pure definition of the word when used as an adjective, I will have to agree. No, it isn't fair.

But it is the way it is, and neither you nor I can change it, no matter how unfair we may think it is. It just *is* and we must accept that fact.

It is not that hard to accept this concept when it involves other people. When the comparisons start involving you personally, humans have a bit more difficulty accepting the same concept and doing so easily.

Look at your life in relation to the lives of those around you. Life will always seem unfair in some way if we want to view it that way. What I am trying to impart to you is that people are not born into this world under even and equal circumstances, so there will never be an even playing field. Therefore, there should be no attempts to turn it into such, or to see it as such.

Now you just need to individualize that understanding down to the level of every aspect of your life, and you will have made a great step forward in terms of life and living it more fully.

You have the ability to change many things in your life and go anywhere and do anything that you can dream, with some advance planning and hard work and a good education. Just don't carry along that burden of the expectation of fairness in life.

It's a weight on your shoulders that you don't need and that will only impede your progress. It will also leave a very bitter taste in your mouth and one that will poison your soul.

The way I see it, "fair" is a noun and brings to mind the annual event in Dallas, Texas known as the "State Fair". Fair as an adjective should never be used to describe life.

In later chapters of this book, I can guarantee you that as you read some of the realities I present to you, that little voice in your head is going to be shouting out "That's not fair," as well it should. That is why I made this the first chapter in this book, so you would have a basis on which to truly understand the things I have chosen to write about. I know that it's all not fair. My goal is to teach you that fact, and the fact that it was never intended to be fair. It just is and one must accept that.

Chapter II.

The Ripple Effect

I'm sure that you, at some time in your life, have thrown a rock into a pond of water. If you have not, by some chance, stop reading now and go fill your bathtub or some large container with water, and find a small pebble, marble or rock. When the tub or container is full and the water is completely calm and resembles a sheet of glass, toss the object into the water. Watch the top of the water carefully and observe what happens.

When the object breaks through the surface of the water, ripples spread out from the spot where the object hit the water, and these ripples continue until they reach the sides of the container, or in a natural body of water, until they reach the shore.

This of course has a scientific explanation and involves many principles, including gravity, density, and other laws and principles of physics, and can be calculated mathematically using algebraic formulas or those found in calculus and higher realms of mathematics.

My purpose is not to go into the technical explanations of what happened when you did this. My purpose is to use this as an example of our life and the things we do. Anything you do in life can be compared to a stone being thrown into a pool of water.

Most people tend to think of any isolated incident as being one stone that hit the water and ended up on the bottom of the pond. Once it is done and over with, it is pretty much forgotten. Forgotten by us and we think by everyone else also.

That, however, is not the case. Everything we do in this life has the same effect as the stone when it breaks the surface of the water. It sends out ripples in every direction and these ripples directly or indirectly touch other people's lives. We may or may not know how and if they are affected in some way by us, but other people are always affected by even our smallest actions.

What you say to someone else, whether kind or unkind, may be something that makes a huge difference in the rest of their lives. Sound absurd? Trust me; it's far from being absurd. You never know what small insignificant word or action of yours may be the thing that gives another person enough hope to keep going or may be the one little thing that makes them give up.

Let me give you an example from an actual event in my past. I was married to a horrible man who abused me both verbally and physically for many years. He spent every penny we made on himself, but expected there to always be enough money to pay for everything. Definitely a situation that wasn't easy to live in. However, that's the way it was. One night he sent me to Taco Bell to get dinner. My 2-year-old daughter went with me. I had not one dollar in my pocket. I was desperate, because to have returned empty-handed would have meant not only hunger for the three of us, but a beating as well. He nearly killed me one time, and I knew he could very well accomplish that without trying too hard, as he was extremely strong and became more so when his anger took over.

I pulled up to the drive-through speaker, ordered, and then pulled up to the window to pay. The man told me it was $9.00 and some change. I rummaged through my purse as if looking for something, then shakily turned to him and told him I left my wallet at home. Could he go ahead and let me take the food, and let me bring him back the money later that evening? I knew I was lying, but as I said I was desperate. He hesitated, but agreed to do so, asking me again if I would bring the money back later that evening. I assured him I would, even though it was a lie. I am not a liar, but when you live in fear of your life on a daily basis, you learn to do whatever it takes to stay alive.

Many years went by. I divorced that man, regained my self-esteem, and because of the experiences of those years, I have grown as a person in ways I would never have expected.

Fast-forward now to ten or twelve years later. I stopped at that same Taco Bell for lunch before an appointment. I saw that same man there, and it turned out he was the manager. I later found out he owns that store and had for about thirteen years.

I asked an employee his name, and after the lunch rush slowed down a bit, I walked up to the counter and asked one of the employees to tell him I wanted to see him.

I asked him how long he had been at that store, and he told me about thirteen years. I asked him if he remembered a young woman with a little girl with her that had ordered food one evening and had supposedly left her wallet at home. She had promised him she would come back that same night and pay him, but had never returned.

He looked at me with a strange look, and said that yes, he remembered such an incident. I handed him a ten dollar bill and told him that now the debt was paid. I also told him thank you. He stood there a minute, and looked at me and said thank you to me, and even told me that it wasn't necessary to pay him. I felt tears forming in my eyes, and I told him that I always paid my debts, and that I had never forgotten his kindness. I also told him that he could never fully understand the extent of what his actions that night had meant to me and my daughter, but that I was finally able to pay him back and I finally had seen him to do so. He thanked me, but I told him he was the one that deserved the thanks.

In all reality, there is a very real possibility that I am alive today in part due to his actions that night. Though he had probably regretted the decision he made until the day I paid him, he will never understand the ramifications of what he did as it affected my life and the lives of those in my household that night.

A very well known law of physics states that "for every action, there is an equal and opposite reaction." That is basically what this is about.

Action and reaction. Cause and effect. Actions and their consequences.

If you don't attend class and you don't do the required work, you won't pass the class. If you steal or kill or assault someone, you will get arrested and charged with the crime and have to pay a debt to society in the form of prison time, probation, parole, etc.

I am about to address something that involves a subject that always gets emotions running high and opinions flying. I am not expressing an opinion for or against this subject, I am strictly informing you of the possible and probable consequences should you decide to take this course of action.

Every young person needs to be very much aware of the sex offender laws that exist in this state of Texas. If someone under the age of eighteen – the age of consent – has sex with anyone, it is illegal. You cannot consent until you are 18. Period.

Let's look at this. Brandon is 19 and is dating Alyssa who is 17. They started having sex a few months ago, and Alyssa is overheard talking to her best friend on the phone by her mother walking down the hall. Thinking her mother is asleep, she isn't being too quiet, and her door is cracked open.

After about five minutes of eavesdropping, her mother asks her to please come in to her bedroom when she gets off the phone. Alyssa has no idea what is getting ready to happen. Do you?

By the time she gets to her mother's room, her mother is visibly angry. She tells Alyssa to sit down and informs her that the police are on the way to their house. Why?

Alyssa's mother is going to have Alyssa sign a statement verifying that she and Brandon have had sexual relations, and then she is going to file charges against Brandon for sexual assault with a minor, or something similar. The consequences are the same.

What you need to realize is that he will be arrested, and will probably be given deferred adjudication, also called probation or community supervision – which will be explained in detail in Chapter 10 – but he will also **be required to register with each and every police department in any city where he lives for the rest of his life as a sex offender.**

In other words, he will be viewed in the same way as the monster who makes child porn videos, or who lurks in the shadows waiting to grab a child and sexually molest them. A pedophile.

Just because Alyssa consented to have sex with Brandon, she is not old enough to do so. He is, but even if he was only 17, he is old enough to be tried as an adult and, being the male, he will be seen as the perpetrator of the crime and the one who will suffer for the rest of his life.

Brandon is "branded" for the rest of his life as a sex offender. His picture will appear on the city police department's web site, and on many other websites that will give you the exact address where every sex offender lives in a specific neighborhood, and very possibly in the local newspaper.

If Brandon moves and doesn't register with the police department, after a certain period of time, they will issue a warrant for his arrest for failure to do so, and he will go to jail again. He will then be considered a greater threat to society and the nightmare goes on and on, and for Brandon, never ends.

If you think I am wrong, call the District Attorney's office and speak to a prosecutor. It happens every day, many times in many different courtrooms.

Another "effect" of sex is pregnancy. DNA testing leaves no doubt as to the identification of a child's father, and child support continues for 18 to 22 years and if a person gets behind in payments, the arrearages are "penalized" at a rate of 6% per year. This obligation never, ever goes away.

If you are going to have sex, be willing to accept any possible consequences for those ten minutes of pleasure. It could cost you either of the above, or even disease or death.

Is ten minutes worth that? No. No. A thousand times no.

You must know that there are many sides to any issue and they all have a different viewpoint. This can be proven very easily if you will have two or three people sit around a table. Person A is sitting across from Person C. Person C can see the things behind Person A that are not in Person A's range of view. Does that mean that they are not there, or that Person C is lying about what they see? No. It just means Person A cannot see them. They are real and they are still there. If each person were to shift one seat in either direction, their viewpoint would change, and include things they couldn't see from the seat they were previously occupying.

However, some things are pretty "cut and dried" and there is only *one* viewpoint and it probably won't be *yours*, at least when it comes to society's rules/laws.

Every word we say can literally change, one way or the other, the course of someone else's life and we may never be aware of it. A smile from a stranger, a compliment to someone we meet in passing, holding the door for an elderly person or a woman with several small children. They seem like nothing to us at the time, but these simple human acts of kindness can have long lasting or even life-changing effects on that stranger who you may never see again, but who may never forget you for that one little thing that made the difference in the rest of their life.

The important thing to remember is that some of our actions that we perform very selfishly and don't even think anyone else notices are sometimes the ones that send another human being down a dark path that we are never aware of. A path of drugs, alcohol, depression, crime or even suicide. Road rage comes to mind as one of the possibilities. Keep in mind every day that what you say and what you do may change the life of someone around you, in a good way or a bad way.

I don't want to scare you into doing nothing. Just the opposite. All I am trying to make you aware of is that we affect the people around us every day with our words and our actions, and we should strive to end each day by looking back and reflecting on the fact that we sent out ripples of beauty, kindness and goodness to those around us, even those we don't know and never will. They may very well be the ones most affected by what we said and did.

It's not an easy task, and I still fail miserably on many occasions. However, the more we try, the easier it gets to realize that "no man is an island" and we all co-exist in this world. We all affect and are affected by those around us, directly or indirectly.

I wrote this book to directly affect you, the reader, in the hope that you can go out into the world and positively affect it and the people that live in it. You have your lives in front of you. The trip is long, and only you can make it a wonderful journey

Every little thing matters. You matter. Your words and your actions matter. The things you don't do also matter. Really think about this. Realize this.

Chapter III.

Balancing a Checkbook

You are probably amused by the title of this chapter, but this simple ability is one that many people just cannot do and do correctly.

How many times have you heard a joke – possibly one about blondes – that says something like this –

"But I can't be out of money, I still have checks!!"

Everyone laughs, but there is more truth to this statement than you would think.

It's a simple concept, but one that even some highly degreed professionals can't manage and perform correctly.

Let's break it down into its smaller elements and go through the entire process. If you are like me and have never seen anything difficult about doing this and doing it efficiently, you are more than welcome to skip to the next chapter. I really won't mind.

When you initially open a checking account, you deposit money into it. Let's say you put $500 into the account to open it.

That amount is recorded as the opening deposit and then carried over to the balance column to let you know your balance, which is the amount of money in the account.

The next day, you go shopping and spend $100 at Target. You write the check at the checkout stand for $100 and then record this check number - 101 - who it was written to – Target – and the amount of the check. You then subtract this $100 from the $500 and you new balance is $400.

Below I am going to list some transactions that occur over the next week or so and then ask you how much you have in your account at the end of the list. Let's see if you can do it.

Check #102 - Walgreen's - $35
Check #103 - Your mother - $50
Deposit your paycheck - $215
Deposit a check from your sister - $40
Check #104 - School - $25
Bank service charge taken out for this month - $11

Now, what is your remaining balance?

Your answer should have been $534. You subtract the checks and add in the deposits.

That sounds easy enough, but there are a few variables that tend to throw people off. I will cover and explain these now.

Calling to check your balance

This is a great way to find out how much money you have, *but you must also find out if any of the checks you have written have not cleared the bank.* If a check is still not paid, then you must subtract that amount to find your actual balance, different from the one you were given over the phone.

Using Debit cards in place of writing checks

The convenience of this is great and it is far less time consuming when you check out. However, you must remember it is the same process as if you had written a check. The money will come out of your account, and much quicker, but it still needs to be recorded in your check register exactly as if you had written a check. One advantage of Debit Cards is that if you don't have enough money in your account to cover your purchase, it won't approve the amount, most of the time. *Not every time, though.*

But if you knew how much money was in there, you shouldn't have tried to spend more than you had. So you see, you must be accountable for your balance.

It is, after all, your money. I know at all times within a few cents how much I have in my checking account, and I rarely record anything at all in the check register. Technology can be thanked for this, in the form of online banking.

I have become the #1 fan of online banking, and I would recommend it to anyone who has ever had even the tiniest problem keeping a checkbook balanced and correctly notated. You can check your balance daily and see what items have cleared and which have not, and even pay your bills through your bank's website, at which time they are deducted from your balance, so there is no lag time/float time for them to clear.

Whether using the listing of my account's activity online or my check register in my checkbook, though, record keeping is absolutely essential in order to keep track of money. Bank fees for overdrafts are outrageous, and at this time average about $33 per returned item. A check will be returned to whom it was written and many times they will present it for payment a second time. If there still is not enough money to pay it, you will be charged another overdraft fee of $33. That means $66 it has cost you to write a check that now will be returned again unpaid.

Usually the place to which you wrote the check will send you a letter requesting payment of the unpaid check. Some companies handle their own returned checks, and many contract with outside collection companies to do this for them.

Either way, there will be a fee involved once again. These fees range from around $7 to around $35 at the time of this writing. So let's do the math here and see what all this really means to you.

Say you write a check to Dillard's for a dress or a suit for a dance and it costs you $234. If this check is returned twice unpaid and ends up in collection, you have already been charged $66 by your bank and then you will have to pay an additional fee of (averaging here only) $21 when you pay the check off so that is $87 in addition to the original amount of $234, for a grand total of $321. Your $234 dress or suit has actually ended up costing you $321.

What most people don't realize is that after the second time a check is returned unpaid by the bank, it can and many times is, forwarded to the County District Attorney's Office for collection. If enough checks from the same person end up there, they can file criminal charges of "Theft by Check" in differing degrees – amounts – and issue a warrant for your arrest.

It is not something pleasant to get your mail out of the mailbox and find a letter from the District Attorney's office telling you that there is a warrant out for your arrest for "hot" checks. Or worse, coming home to find a Sheriff's Officer's business card stuck in your front door, which means they have been there looking for you.

When this happens, you can either call a bondsman and go down and be booked in, fingerprinted, have your mug shot taken, and then released on bond, or you can go through the same procedure and pay off the entire amount of the outstanding checks.

However, the thing is that once a warrant is issued, it doesn't go away by just paying off the checks. You have to be arrested and go through the booking procedure in order to cancel the warrant out of the system. The charges will be dropped, but the arrest cannot be avoided.

Sometimes and in some places, this can be accomplished quickly, being known as a "walk-through". However, in some places, this is not possible, and you might have to be put through the same procedure as any of the other people being booked in to the jail, and the entire process may take up to eight hours or more. Most of this time will be spent in a "holding cell" with all the other lovely people that are being arrested for anything from public intoxication to murder, and most of them are not happy about being there and are not likely to be friendly. Especially when you are dressed in nice clothes and obviously come from a middle-class or higher socioeconomic background.

And all because you couldn't balance your checkbook. Definitely not worth it!

If a person can add and subtract, with or without a calculator, then there is no reason beyond laziness that the average person, young or old, cannot keep a balanced checkbook and know at any given time how much money *is available to spend.*

Once a check is written, consider that money gone. The reality is that it may take up to a week or more for a check to actually "clear" your account and the money be taken out, but if you will consider the money *gone* the minute you write the check, you shouldn't have too many problems.

I'm not saying that there will not be an occasional mistake, such as forgetting to record a check or Debit Card purchase, or even recording a deposit twice. I personally have been guilty of both. However, these occasional mistakes are not catastrophic enough in nature to cause you more than a few problems, but at $33 per "problem," the expense adds up quickly.

Get in the habit of balancing your checkbook when you receive your statement. This really is a very easy task. Place a checkmark in your check register beside all the checks that have cleared on that statement, and do the same thing for all the deposits. Record, deduct from your balance, and check off any service charges/monthly fees that appear on the statement. If this is not visual enough for you to be able to easily figure out, highlight the paid items and that will leave the outstanding items clearly visible in your check register.

Now take what you show as your current balance and *add in* any checks that have not been checked off, and *subtract* any deposits made that haven't been checked off.

The figure you get after you do this should be what your current balance is on the statement. If it's not, find the difference, and look for that amount somewhere that you may have missed, or possibly an old check that still hasn't cleared and you forgot about, or something similar. Usually the amount will be easy to find as it matches something in your check register. It may even be a monthly service charge you forgot to record, though this would have made your previous statement out of balance. Also be aware that it is likely that an amount was recorded wrong in the check register. A check for $62.14 may have been written down as $64.12, and you don't have to suffer from dyslexia for this to happen. The important thing is to find the error, and balance the checkbook to the bank statement. Get someone else to look at it if you can't find the difference. If this doesn't solve the problem, go to your local branch bank and ask someone there to help you with it. They will be more than happy to assist you.

Balancing and keeping a checkbook is really one of the simplest things to do if you record every transaction in or out of the account and consider the money gone the minute the transaction is completed or the check is written. Reconciling with your statement each month will take only a couple of minutes and is a small amount of time to invest to make sure there are no bank errors – and yes, they do make mistakes – and any problems can be taken care of immediately.

You keep up with schedules of classes and tests and practices and rehearsals and more. Keeping up with your money is no harder, and much more important now and for your future well-being. Money is necessary in order to live in this world, and you don't want to waste it or needlessly give it to someone else because you couldn't pay enough attention to avoid overdrawing your account.

It's simple math and nothing more. You can do it. I know you can! If you can pass elementary school, then you can balance a checkbook. And that is the truth!

Once again, you can do anything you want to do badly enough. It just requires time and effort.

Chapter IV.

Entitlement

Let's refer to Miriam-Webster for a definition of this word. Entitle means "to furnish with proper grounds for seeking or claiming something." Entitlement is the "belief that one is deserving of or entitled to certain privileges."

There is an attitude among many people in this country, especially the younger generations, that this world owes them something just because they live in it.

Let me take a minute to laugh, please. If you are of this same belief, please take a few minutes and answer the following questions for me.

When you were born into this world, what did you have? Nothing. Absolutely nothing.

Up to the day you read this, what have you accumulated in this world that you have earned or paid for yourself? This answer will vary, but if you are not old enough to work, then the answer more than likely will be nothing or very little.

What makes you any different from anyone else that you would think someone should treat you differently – better – than the person sitting beside you? If you actually had the audacity to start listing things, write them down now and then continue reading.

Let's see if I can guess some of the possible answers that might have been given. Prettier, richer, smarter, more popular, cooler. I sincerely hope that many of you reading this did not list any answers other than the obvious correct one, which is "nothing."

The hard truth of the matter is that no matter how rich, pretty, cool or popular you may think you are now, there is still nothing this world or society owes you, and plenty you owe it. You are entitled to nothing just because you live and breathe. You are nothing special, and if you think you are, you are sadly mistaken.

Now let me say that each of us is special. Granted, we are each unique and possess unique talents and gifts. But as far as being "special" in the eyes of this world, you can and should forget it, and do it now.

I heard that students are entering college and demanding "A"s in their classes, reasoning that since they are paying to be there, they deserve an "A." I have never heard such a ridiculous notion in my entire life.

You are rewarded in this life according to the effort you put into whatever avenue you pursue. If you believe that you can slack your way through life and expect to get rich, you are in for a rude awakening.

Learn this now and know that it is true!

The federal governmental attitude in this country is that each and every child deserves an education. That is something I agree with. However, that child has to take advantage of the opportunity and apply themselves and learn the material that is presented to them.

Just because there is a law on the books that says all children will be given the chance to go to school, the schools in no way owe that child anything more than to provide the teachers in the classrooms to present the material, giving them the opportunity to learn it.

Grades have to be earned by each individual student just the same as salaries are earned by each individual person in the workforce.

Get ready for the little voice to start shouting in your head. There are many stupid people making a lot of money and there are a lot of really smart people making very little money in this world. No, it is not fair, and no one said it ever would be. However, both the stupid person and the smart person must go to work and be there at the assigned times. They must perform their job satisfactorily for their superiors, and if they do these things, they will both get paid. If either or both fail to do these things, they will be fired and will be making nothing.

It's a very simple concept, but one that is not being taught to the younger generations in this country, or maybe one they just fail to understand *really* does apply to each and every one of them.

Not a one of you is so special that the world or society will give you a thing just because you are who you are. Don't expect it, and please don't be disappointed when it doesn't happen. Each and every one of you will have to be accountable for the things you do and don't do, and if you believe that you can still be partying and "hanging out" when you are 25 or 26 and your parents will still be handing over money for gas and beer and clothes, you need to come back to earth and plant your feet on the hard ground and do a reality check. I'm not saying it doesn't happen, but the one word that comes to mind is "worthless."

This one I can speak about from personal experience. Details are not necessary, but it finally gets to a point where a parent will wash their hands of a child that never sees fit to work, contribute to the household, and continually expects to be given whatever money or material things they think they need, and who even has the nerve to get mad if they aren't immediately given whatever they ask for. In this case, the adult child just decided to take everything of any value the parent had, stealing over $40,000 of heirloom jewelry and everything electronic that could be pawned for $20, including all the children's DVDs that the younger kids had. They of course, destroyed the home to make it look like an outsider had come in, and nearly killed the parent in the process, mentally and physically, due to the emotional aftermath.

What you do determines what you get. You came in to this world naked and with nothing, and you will leave this world the same way. What you do in between is totally up to you, but the world owes you nothing, and it would be best for everyone if you learned this truth now and never forget it.

You are entitled to nothing, but you are capable of anything. It won't be given to you but there is nothing that isn't available to you if you are willing to work for it and do what it takes to make it happen. Your future is an empty canvas on which you can paint the life of your dreams. Just remember you have to buy the paints and the brushes in order to be able to paint your own personal masterpiece – your life. There is no shame in occasionally needing and asking for help, but where you go and what you achieve in life is mostly up to you and you alone.

Chapter V.

Free

What does the word "free" mean to you? Think about this a moment. Some of the most common answers are -
    Without cost
    Not tied down
    Not confined
    No charge

We learn that the United States of America is a free country. Compared to many other countries in the world, we are extremely lucky to live without being under the thumb of a tyrannical government. We enjoy many freedoms that make this the destination of people from all over the world because of the opportunities our type of government affords its citizens.

However, are we really free? Not hardly. We all have to adhere to the rules set forth by not only the federal government, but each state has its own laws, and then each city or municipality further restricts our freedoms by making laws as to what each individual can and cannot do.

Now, this is not in and of itself a bad thing. Society has to have rules of conduct by which its people must live. Otherwise, there would be chaos, and no way to control it.

However, think about all this purely in the terms of being free. You aren't free to do too much except what everyone else does, because if you do, someone will punish you for not following the rules. Cut class, get detention, suspension, and/or fail the class. Drive on the wrong side of the road, and if you don't get killed or kill someone else, you get a ticket and/or wreck your car. Have your garage band practice at 3 AM in your driveway, and the police will show up and you will be told to stop and possibly issued a citation.

My point is that we are free in this country to do things that fall under the category of acceptable behaviors, but we are not totally free. We are not now, never have been, and never will be.

Another idea of free is getting something for nothing. Believe me, **there is nothing free in this world**. Everything comes at some cost.

The internet has provided more opportunities to trick people with "free" offers than any other type of media, and please note that every time you see some "Free" offer for dinner, a shopping spree, a laptop, or a car, there is always this little symbol following the word "free" and it is "*". The asterisk.

That little asterisk is there to tell you that there is a catch of some kind. In other words, there are conditions and restrictions or costs involved in the "free" offer. And that automatically makes it *not free.*

There is no one in this world that will give you a free laptop just because you logged on to play some game on some website. You and everyone else in the world that's been to that same site for the last two or three days has gotten that same message. Don't think you are special or lucky. The advertisers pay exorbitant amounts of money to place the ads offering "free" things to anyone with a computer who will do just about anything to try to get something free. They put that asterisk there and in small print at the very bottom of the ad you will find the words "*see offer details" or "*some restrictions apply."

That's calling a mountain lion a kitten! If you have ever looked at some of the details, they can and are most of the time virtually impossible to fulfill in the manner they describe, so therefore, you couldn't ever get that free dinner for two, or that laptop, or that vacation package. But, in the process, they have had you apply for credit, giving them vital important information about you like your Social Security number, address, and much other information that now can be shared, sold, or even stolen and used by someone other than you to obtain credit or even steal your identity.

I am not saying that all these companies that make the offers of some type of freebie are dishonest, but if you have to obtain a credit card and spend so much each month on it, buy a certain number of CDs from a record club, and then buy so many gallons of gas at a certain gas station for the next 6 months in order to receive a card that is good for dinner for two at Chili's, then that dinner just cost you hundreds or thousands of dollars, if you were able to complete the requirements. What if you couldn't get the credit card because you had no credit or bad credit? There goes the free dinner right there.

My point is that there is an old saying that says "there is a sucker born every minute." I would bet that number has increased! Please don't be one of these suckers.

Know that there is nothing truly free in this world. Everything that appears to be free will usually have some strings attached. With one very obvious exception.

There is only one thing I know of that could truly be considered free. Educational grants for college. Pell Grants and some state grants are awarded to college students who meet certain financial requirements and these grants do not have to be paid back, but only if certain requirements are met. The student must maintain a certain GPA, they must complete the course of study they have chosen within a certain time frame and this money doesn't pay for classes that are not part of the chosen degree plan.

In other words, you have to do what is required of you to keep and use the free money. Strings attached? Yes. But who would realistically expect it to be any other way?

Except those who feel entitlement. And those who are still screaming that life isn't fair. I thought we took care of those problems already. Maybe some of you need to go back and re-read the first part of the book again, and maybe again, and maybe again.

If you read it enough times, perhaps it will soak in and start to take root. We can only hope.

Chapter VI.

Paying Attention

There is not one single person reading this that has not heard someone tell them to "Pay attention!" This is something you hear from the time you are a small child. There is always the "dreamer" in every class who is always being told to pay attention to the teacher. This involves hearing as well as looking at something or someone.

This is one of the most important things you really need to learn how to do well in life. Not just in a classroom, but every day and every minute you are awake. Paying *real* attention. Some are born with the ability to do this quite naturally, but for some it is a learned response to the massive amounts of stimuli that surrounds each of us each and every day.

A word of advice – **learn to do this to the best of your ability and start practicing immediately in order to sharpen your skills to their very finest in the shortest possible time period.**

Why?

The reasons are numerous, but well worth the time to set forth for you here.

Obviously, you can't learn if you don't pay attention. If your lips are moving, then you can't be paying attention to anything but what you are saying. If what you are saying was something everyone needed to know, you would be in front of the classroom instead of in one of the student seats.

School is something you need to take very seriously. You should make every effort to absorb as much of the knowledge presented to you as you can, and go out and learn as much more as you can along the way.

Knowledge is power.

That statement carries more truth in just three words than probably any other I have ever read or heard.

Another reason to pay attention is to stay out of trouble or to avoid becoming a victim of a crime.

People get mugged, robbed, kidnapped and/or killed daily. I have been a victim of crimes myself. However, I know from these experiences that I am alive today because I was alert to what was happening and to my surroundings. This gave me the ability to manipulate the direction the crime took in a number of ways, and I came out of it alive. It is absolutely necessary to remain calm and collected while being victimized, so that you can remember details that the police will need later in order to solve the crime. It also may be the one thing that means you live through it. There is plenty of time after the fact to fall apart and cry and actually feel the fear from what has just happened to you. However, during the event, shift all your senses into high gear and burn the events into your memory for later reference.

Let me give you an example of paying attention. You should be able to know if the way another person is acting seems out of place or unusual or suspicious. I was at the grocery store recently and I noticed a scruffy-looking man enter the store. I then saw him leave the store running out the door. A few minutes later, he was back inside and was talking with a woman who was using the self checkout lane. When I left, he was walking out the door the same time as I was. As I put my things in the back of my car, I noticed he was parked in an old run-down pickup in the striped areas at the front of the parking lot where parking is not allowed. The woman was beside him in the truck. Before I finished, he backed down the aisle I was parked on and pulled in a parking spot across from me and turned the truck off. He got out and was rummaging around in the back of the truck, as if waiting for someone or something.

Do you consider his behavior normal? I would hope not. In addition to his strange in-and-out behavior, he was out of place due to his appearance.

Most people probably wouldn't have noticed all of this, but I can tell you it is in your best interest if you will pay real attention to what goes on around you and the people involved.

When something doesn't seem right, it probably isn't. If you don't feel comfortable in a situation or around a certain person, there is probably reason you shouldn't.

Each of us has a little voice that alerts us to something we should be wary of if we will just listen to it and realize that it is trying to protect us. Call it instinct, attribute it to some higher power, call it a "gut feeling." What you call it and where you think it comes from are irrelevant. What is important is that you listen to it and not have to have a reason why. You may never know why you just didn't get out of the house on time, or why you just couldn't continue down that street that night when you were walking home. If something inside of you says not to do something, then just don't.

Women tend to heed this little voice more naturally than men, but I can tell you that it won't ever steer you into harm's way. If you will listen to it, you will probably be prevented from harm of some kind. Though you may never know what could have happened, the fact that nothing did happen should be enough for anyone.

Here's a true story about this. Ray loved to fly and owned a small plane with one of his friends. One evening he went straight from work to the airport, and prepared the plane to fly. However, he went to the airport office, and chatted with the men there, and for whatever reasons that later he said he couldn't explain, he wasted enough time that it got dark and he went home. He didn't fly, and he said something just kept nagging at him making him feel that he shouldn't get in that plane and take off.

About three days later, the co-owner of the plane called him and told him that he had just that day had to make an emergency landing in a field only a short distance from the airport as the engine stalled and wouldn't start again. Had Ray flown the night he planned to but didn't, he would have taken off in the opposite direction and would have been directly over the downtown area when the engine quit. There would have been no place for him to safely land.

He listened to that little voice. He is extremely glad he did.

Pay attention to your teachers, your parents, your car, your surroundings, and everything happening to you at every moment of your life. It may be crucial to remember something at a future date that, had you been paying attention, would have been no problem to recall. However, if you weren't paying attention, you therefore wouldn't be able to remember.

There have been numerous kidnapped individuals found alive due to a total stranger noticing something that seemed unusual or suspicious and alerting the police. Had someone not been paying attention, these victims could very well have been dead had they not been found when they were.

I believe you see what I am trying to tell you. Knowing and doing are two separate things though. This particular habit takes practice, and is developed over time. But the advantages of sharpening the skill of truly seeing who and what is around you are too numerous to list and are priceless. I can't think of another learned response that can and will prove to be as valuable to you as this one.

Besides, you have a dream and goals for your life. Paying attention will only help you on your way, and may make the journey more pleasant. You won't miss as much and may notice something or someone that will change your life.

Your life will never be any worse because you truly paid attention.

Chapter VII.

Popular

Let's get the definition of this from the dictionary. "Commonly liked or approved." A synonym given is "common."

"Popular" is such a thing of importance in the halls of the schools in this country, and even second-graders can be heard while at play discussing which of their Barbie dolls is popular and which ones are not.

The concept of "popular" can be found on many shows for young people that air daily on the various cable and satellite stations, such as Disney and Nickelodeon. Recently, there was even a Disney Channel movie about the subject, in which a young girl's personal journal became a bestseller. In it, her alter ego put the popular crowd in its place, and was unconcerned with who they thought they were. The girl's personal dreams of popularity were realized for a short period of time until she made it known that all her characters were based on actual people in her school. That was a recipe for disaster, though the truth of what she said about all of them was evident. Truth hurts sometimes.

So does popularity and the importance it is afforded among the student bodies.

Most groups of the "popular" in any given school are far from "commonly liked." In fact, they usually are the most undignified, rude and haughty of the entire group.

Many times they are the cheerleaders, football players, and others who may or may not stand out in some way for their achievements, even if these are rarely academic.

Many times, their socioeconomic background plays a factor in their so-called popularity, but there are many factors, and the factors may change some over time.

"Common" and "popular" are among a group of synonyms that are discussed in the dictionary as "generally met with and not in any way special, strange, or unusual."

I find it amusing as well as affording a bit of justification that the word "vulgar" was among this particular group of synonyms in this particular dictionary.

That is closer in my opinion to the proper way to describe the whole "popular" thing going on in our schools.

The one question that needs to be answered is –

Just who are these popular people popular with?

The only answer is - each other.

Popularity in school is no more than a group of people, through association or socioeconomic class, who see themselves as better and more wonderful than the other members of the student body. How this monster comes to life at some point on the educational trail is somewhat shrouded in mystery. But once the little cliques involved pledge allegiance to their popularity, the monster comes to life and becomes bigger than the sum of its parts.

How many lives have been changed by this is something no one will ever know. However, from each adult's past experiences with popularity, whether from within the golden circle or most likely from outside its boundaries, the answer is far too many. It is common knowledge that those who make up the popular segment of the school populations are known for their feelings of superiority, and are very vocal in their disapproval of the more "lowly" they are forced to associate with each day.

Geeks, nerds, anyone not among their elite ranks, are snubbed, verbally abused, and regularly told how inferior they are. One of the newest terms heard for this behavior is "laming on" them.

Self-esteem is something that is precariously perched in place at this time in a person's life, and with the onset of puberty sits even more shakily on its perch.

"Popular" takes what little self-esteem there may be in some children and knocks it to the ground, and then proceeds to grind it into the dirt. Having personally seen many wonderful young people crushed under the snobbery of the "elite" popular on a daily basis, I can't help but wonder the effects of this for the rest of these children's lives.

What do you think the underlying reason was behind the Columbine shootings? Was not the same thing responsible for the Virginia Tech killing spree? Read up on these if unfamiliar with them, please.

I believe you understand this, especially if you are still in school. To those of you who are the "popular" among you, I am not against you. However, you must refer back to the chapter on the "ripple effect" and realize that due to your status as "popular", the truths of that concept should especially be considered when acting or speaking to those around you.

The final aspect of popularity is one that will come as quite a surprise. After high school, you will not be popular with anyone any more. As each of you goes off to a different college or career path, you will no longer be "popular."

The "popular" really are only popular among themselves. In fact, they are not held in high regard by the greater majority of those who are not considered "popular." In fact, many are actually disliked even by their teachers and educators.

Wouldn't it be wonderful if the "popular" were also the most highly accredited academically, the most concerned with the well-being of their fellow students, and the ones that everyone enjoyed being around? The hard truth is that these groups are the ones that belittle, bully, and horribly condemn those with whom they journey through their education that they feel are less valuable than they are. The small minority "lames on" the large majority. How totally absurd.

Popular groups need to remember this. There may come a day in the future when you meet again one of the geeks or nerds you used to laugh at and make fun of every day. He/she may turn out to be your new boss, or the person making the hiring decisions at the company you really want to work for. Possibly at some point even one of your children's teachers.

Unfortunately, "popular" is a part of school and a part of every student's life, at least until graduation from high school. Then, I guarantee you, it will end. There are no such groups on college campuses as the "populars", for which I am grateful.

Their days are numbered. Unfortunately, the monster lives and seems to be born much earlier in the twelve-year journey through school with each passing year. To those that are "popular," I have offered my advice. To the other 98% of the students in schools everywhere, I offer you the following truths.

> No one can make you feel any way except the way you allow yourself to feel. It is not what is said to you that matters, it is how you react to it.

> It is not the name you are called, but whether you choose to believe it or not.

Today there seems to be a focus on school campuses on bullying and attempts to keep it out of the schools and off their campuses. The bullies and their issues need to be addressed, but I fear they have been unwittingly given a role model by which to bully and which is freely allowed. "Popular" students continue to discriminate and downgrade and humiliate those who are not quite as pretty, rich, or athletic as they are.

Knowledge is power. For those within the circle and those without, would it be asking too much to really try to forge better working relationships with fellow students without having to criticize, tease, or in some way promote feelings of inferiority? Couldn't you minimize your feelings of superiority and refrain from hurting another in the attempt to show how much better you think you are?

Learning to do this now would be better than later.

Because you will have to do this when you get out in the real world and don't have your little clique around you to agree with you or laugh with you when you humiliate someone.

In the real world your "popularity" doesn't exist, and isn't something you can put on a resume. It is worthless, now and later.

The damage it does is much larger than the monster itself, and parents and educators should make any and all efforts to get this point across at the earliest possible age. Lives could be changed, and many might actually be saved.

Wouldn't that be worth the effort? Wouldn't that be more important?

The really important things in life are those being taught by your teachers, your parents, and people like me. Set your sights on learning, helping those who need help, and becoming a person you can look at in the mirror and like.

Everything else, including "popular," will fall by the wayside eventually, but these things remain with you your entire life. Concentrate on your effects on the world, and consider them seriously, and then act accordingly.

If this accords you some type of "popularity", well so be it. However, if it doesn't, so be it. As I stated, this "popularity" shall pass. Please don't let it be a part of who you really are and how you see yourself.

Most important, don't let it affect how you treat others. Treat others in a way that you yourself would want to be treated, and in doing this, you can never go wrong.

Chapter VIII.

Looking Ahead

In this chapter, I will show you some very important reasons for looking ahead and planning for the years ahead.

At the stage of life where most of you are, asking you to look ahead probably means in your mind the end of high school or graduating from college. That is normal and age-appropriate.

However, to older adults and senior citizens, that same period in life is remembered as a real beginning and one that initiates the process of planning for things that are decades away, for that will eventually be where you will arrive in life.

Saving for the future is a concept that most of you will think is not necessary at your age, but one that each and every student in this country should make an effort to do, no matter how small of an amount.

Using an equation for cash accumulation I found on the internet, and which can be found in numerous textbooks and those available at the library, let's show you an example of what I mean.

You have $500 you wish to put into a savings account. You open the account and are able to add an additional $500 per year to this account. That only figures out to $41.66 per month, and I intentionally have used smaller figures. The interest rate of 4.5% in this example never changes, and you never withdraw any money from this account for 40 years. Under these circumstances, which are for example only, at the end of 40 years, the balance in the account would be $59,132.02.

If you chose instead to go shopping with that $500 and you did the same with the yearly amounts of $500, then you would have absolutely nothing at the end of 40 years.

I realize you may not understand the absolute necessity of starting to save for the future. Don't feel too bad. There are many people who are within only ten or fifteen years of retirement age that still haven't started saving for the future. It is just something that we either plan on starting to do next month, or it seems that there just isn't enough money to be able to put some in savings.

Now for a reality check, and I sincerely hope that by the time you younger readers are put in a position to have to handle this for either parents or for yourself, things will be drastically different. At the time I am writing this, though, the figures I am about to show you are accurate and increasing regularly.

For comparison purposes, I will throw out a few figures so there will be a sense of relativity here. In other words, you can't understand the absurdity of one without understanding the others.

Each of you lives somewhere, and for this example we will use a house valued on today's real estate market at $150,000. For ease of example, your monthly mortgage would be $1,500. The car you drive is financed and your monthly payment is $500.

Your grandmother is having health issues and is going to live in a nursing home. She has decided she wants a private room, but will have to take a semi-private room for a couple of months until a private room becomes available.

How much do you think this will cost her? Get ready for the answer.

The semi-private room in a skilled nursing facility will be approximately $4300 per month for her half of the room, and when she moves into the private room, she will have to pay approximately $6500 monthly for it.

Very likely, she will be totally responsible for the entire amount, unless she has long-term care insurance. Most people don't yet. They think Medicare will pay for it. *They are wrong!*

Do you know how big the house would be if your mortgage payments were $6500 per month? You would be extremely wealthy if you could afford and qualify for a mortgage like that. Extremely wealthy!

Unless there is some planning and saving done throughout your life, and the earlier you start the better, you could reach the final years of your life and end up living in poverty or worse.

With expenses like those paid for nursing home care, most of us probably will anyway, because it doesn't take long for even large amounts of money to be depleted at the rate of $6500 per month.

That rate will continue to rise as inflation causes prices to rise. Food prices go up, energy rates increase, insurance rates rise, and the list goes on. These increases are met and resolved through one method - raising the cost of each resident's monthly obligation, and doing so whenever it is felt to be necessary. They have to make a profit, after all.

We as a society have become a throw-away group of people. This has evolved over the last four or five decades, and doesn't seem to show cause for change at any time in the future. Material possessions come and go and if something gets a bit outdated, you just go buy a new one. Even if you don't need it, buy it anyway because you want one or because someone else has one and you think you need one too.

Having grown up as most of you have, there is probably nothing I can say or show you that will have much effect on your view of buying or shopping, or about the value of anything.

When I ask you to look ahead, I want you to be aware that the day will come when you are not working, or can't work, or retire to enjoy the rest of your life. When that happens, you will still have monthly obligations that require money. Will you be able to meet those obligations? Is there some money in a bank account somewhere that has been growing so that if you lost your job you could live until you found another one?

Prices keep going up everywhere. When I started driving at the age of sixteen, gas was about 35 cents a gallon. At eighteen, the price reached 50 cents. I remember a dollar a gallon, and until just a few years ago, a gallon of gas had never cost more than $1.80. However, in the early summer of 2008, a gallon of gas cost $4.00 per gallon, having increased about $2.20 per gallon within just a few weeks.

Did anyone get any type of increase in their wages to balance this increase? Of course not. Wages stayed the same for everyone and were not raised to offset this increase in gasoline prices. If you used twenty gallons of gas a week to commute to work, then you had been spending approximately $36 per week on gas. All of a sudden, you were spending $80 per week. That represents an increase of $44 per week, and $156 per month. Yet your paycheck stays the same. Surprises like this happen all the time in life. All I want you to do is be aware that these things do indeed happen, and that you will be directly affected by them.

The more prepared you can be for these little surprises, the easier your life will be.

One more thought about looking ahead. The females reading this are so extremely lucky to be able to choose any career in the world and be able to achieve that goal. The women of the world have only had this ability for less than fifty years. The doors have opened and opportunity abounds in every field.

Never in the history of the world have women been afforded such opportunity to excel and to be whatever they want to be. You girls have no idea how limited the future appeared for your mothers, grandmothers, and every other generation before you.

Set your goals and meet or exceed them. You are not bound by the social conventions and taboos of the past, so don't hold yourself back. Do what you want to do and be what you want to be.

You are reaping the rewards of the seeds planted and tended by centuries of women before you. When you succeed, then their efforts were not in vain or for nothing.

The future stretches ahead of you, sometimes seemingly endlessly. Change the world and have fun doing it.

Chapter IX.

Learn, Learn, Learn

I realize that for many of you school is not your favorite place.

That has always been the case, and probably always will. However, the value of an education cannot be stressed enough, especially in the times we live in.

In order to make a good living, you *must* have a degree of some kind. As strange as that may sound to you, it is the absolute truth. Twenty or thirty years ago, that was not the case, but in today's highly competitive workforce, trust me when I say that one must have some type of college degree in order to earn good money.

On the other side of the coin, not everyone who has a college degree can be considered intelligent. From personal experience, I have known several individuals that had a four-year college degree and could have taught my child in an elementary school that were so stupid everyone wondered how they made it to work and back each day without leaving a trail of bread crumbs so that they wouldn't get lost. There will always be those people and it still remains a mystery to me how they manage to make it through four years of college and make grades high enough to get a degree.

What you must realize is that most colleges grade each class on a point system. You don't receive letter grades on each assignment. You receive a certain number of points for each item the professor requires.

The points are then accumulated throughout the semester and the total determines your final grade. Let me give you an example.

Your class has a total of 1500 possible points for all the assignments. The grades are figured at the end of the semester as follows –

1350 – 1500 = A
1200 – 1349 = B
1050-1199 = C
1000 – 1049 = D
999 and below = F

College classes offer a bit more freedom to the students, as there is the ability to actually skip an assignment, or just not do it, or choose not to take the time to complete nearly any assignment you so desire.

The only ramification of this is that you will lose however many points that assignment would have given you. Thus, you lose that particular number of points. This, of course, can and does greatly affect your final grade.

You are the only one responsible for your grade, no matter if it's elementary school, high school, or college. You don't "deserve" anything other than what you earn.

Learning is a lifelong process. You should make it a habit to try to learn something new each and every day of your life. The day you stop learning is the day you may as well lay down and die.

There is a never-ending supply of information in the world, and with today's technology, it is available to you via the internet. What a wonderful learning tool! Just fifteen or twenty years ago, the information was all still available, but many times it was very hard to find and sometimes harder to access. Libraries and their reference sections were one of the best places to get much of the information you students now take for granted as being available to you with just a few keystrokes and a couple of minutes of your time.

Hopefully you have become aware of the fact by this point in your education that there is a lot of junk on the internet, and unless you get something from a reliable source, you should verify its validity.

An advantage of being a student, especially when you get to college, is that you have access to the libraries of colleges and cities across the country, both in person and via the internet. This is absolutely awesome, and the information in valid, real, and reliable.

You really are lucky to be able to have all this information so readily available to you. *So use it.*

Knowledge is power.

Yes, I have said that previously and I can't stress the importance of those three little words and the concept they embody.

Whatever you decide to do or be, learn more about it than anyone else, and be the best that you can be. Continue to learn about your chosen field. Many careers require continuing education in order to retain your license, certification, or title. But even if yours doesn't, continue to learn and expand your knowledge of your chosen career.

A person can never know too much.

Your brain never gets full.

And as the population of this country ages, at some time in your future, you will personally witness the aging of someone close to you, and you will realize another truth that applies to muscle of any kind - brain or brawn. That truth is that if you don't use it you will lose it.

Learn, learn, and learn some more. Make it a daily habit, during the summer, and after you complete your formal education.

Some excellent ways to daily expand your knowledge are to read a newspaper, read books on anything that interests you, or put a few "word of the day" items on your home page on your computer.

When you walk across that college stage and start making your way in life, the classroom studies may have ended, but then the process of learning truly begins and it continues, each and every day of the rest of your life.

Enjoy it and make it fun. Make it a part of who you are.

Chapter X.

Our Ju$tice $y$tem

I have saved this chapter for the end of the book for a reason. This chapter is going to ruffle the feathers of a lot of people. Educators, professionals in the legal field, and those who haven't experienced the reality of being inside the system - caught in the web and doing your best to get out with the least amount of damage to you and your future. Everything I put forth, therefore, is based on verifiable, actual case histories and can be proven in its entirety.

Our justice system was created by the founding fathers of this country as a better way to govern, and to deal with those who break the law. Breaking away from being ruled by a single person, the ideas and theoretical functions of this system are beautiful in their ideology.

It must be remembered, though, that laws are written from a generalized point of view, and are then interpreted and applied from a specific point of view. Interpretation of any and every law can and does change, and that must be stressed repeatedly and always remembered when dealing with legal matters.

I'm going to present four different situations and how these situations turned out. All involve laws, law enforcement, and the justice (judicial) system. Once again, I will say that these are based on actual experiences of actual people within the last few years in Texas. After reading these, you can decide for yourself if you think justice was served or if there are huge gaping holes in the fabric of this system.

Situation 1.

Jay and Sara have been dating for a number of months. They have a huge argument, and Sara decides to go to his house and try to talk to him. She arrives, walks to the door and rings the doorbell. While she is waiting for him to answer, he sneaks around the side of the house and jumps up behind her, placing his arm in a stranglehold around her neck and dragging her backwards.

She of course is frightened and begins to have trouble breathing as he is choking her. She manages to feel around in her purse and find a pocket knife she always carries with her. She gets it in her hand and drops her purse in the process. She opens it up and cuts Jay's forearm with it. The pain was enough to make him let her go and she ran to her car. He glares at her and grabs her purse, removing her cell phone and throwing the purse on the ground in front of her. He yells at her that he is keeping the phone just in case she was planning to call the police.

The cut on his arm is bleeding, but is only a surface wound that is not deep enough for medical attention, and not really bad enough to require a Band-Aid.

Scared, and shaking badly, Sara drives to a convenience store nearby and calls "911" from the pay phone in the parking lot. Officers arrive shortly, and she tells them the story. She is starting to bruise on her shoulder and one of her arms from the struggle with Jay. Her neck is still red from having his arms tightly around it and she is visibly upset and still shaking and crying. One of the police officers leaves and goes to Jay's house to talk to him.

A few minutes later the officer returns, and pulls the other officer aside and they talk for a couple of minutes. They then both approach Sara. What do you think happens next?

Logically, and taking into consideration the implied protections our laws afford us, it would be safe to think that they tell Sara that Jay is going to be arrested, or they need a written statement from her in order to file charges against him, or something similar. Is this not what you thought would happen? After all, she was the one who was attacked and all she did was defend herself, which is a right afforded the citizens of this country under the law. It is better known as the concept of self-defense. And don't forget that he also stole her cell phone. Theft, though probably not a felony in this case due to the dollar value of the piece of equipment, is still a crime, and did occur.

The actual outcome of this story will surprise you, as well it should. The officer asks Sara if there is anyone that could come get her car and take it home. She says her mother could, but asks why that would be necessary. He removes his handcuffs from his belt and asks her to turn around. She screams. She is being arrested for assault with a deadly weapon, and Jay is not going to be charged with anything. In fact, he is the victim as they see it.

About 6-8 hours later and after paying a bondsman $400 to post her bail, she is released from the city jail. For various reasons that are not relevant to the point this story is trying to make, actual charges are never filed on her for this offense. However, the $400 is never seen again, and never is, and the arrest will still always be on her criminal record, which in Texas, is maintained by the Texas Department of Public Safety.

You can't say the money was wasted, but bond money is never returned to you when bail is arranged through a bondsman. The only way bond money is every returned to someone is if someone posts the *entire amount of the bond* with the court. When you appear for your first court date as ordered, then you will be reimbursed the money you paid for the bond. However, most people do not have that type of money available that can sit in someone else's hands for a few months, so they call a bondsman.

The $400 in this case probably was for an actual bond amount of $2000. Bail bondsmen normally require 20% of the bond amount to be paid before they will actually arrange to get someone out of jail. After a person's release, they must report to the bond office, fill out a long sheet of personal and contact information, and then call in at least once a week to the bond office in order to prevent the bondsman from revoking the bond and having them sent back to jail.

If someone out on bond fails to appear in court as ordered, the judge can - and in most instances does - revoke the bond, and the bond office has to pay the entire amount of the original bond to the court. In other words, the person who got bonded out has now cost that bondsman several thousand dollars. I am wandering off the intended path, and you can verify the exact procedure when there is a bond forfeiture if you so desire with a little research, so let's go back to the situation above.

The victim of assault and theft calls the police and ends up getting arrested and charged with a felony worse than the one exacted on her, and the person who attacked her is made out to be the victim. **This is a real event with real people that actually happened within the last two years in one of the largest cities in the state of Texas.**

That little voice shouting at you about "fair" is getting pretty loud, I know.

Situation 2.

Cindy and David are living together. They have frequent arguments and tonight is no exception. However, David has been drinking beer for hours, and as the fighting escalates, slaps Cindy to the ground. He then begins kicking her and after a few seconds, she gets up and takes a large hardback book off the table by the couch and hits him in the head with it. He goes down, and she then jumps on him and starts hitting him in the face.

He grabs her arm, nearly breaking it but just bruising it. She bloodies his nose and cuts his cheek. She has several small cuts and bruises from where he kicked her and is bleeding from numerous places up and down her body.

She gets up off of him and runs outside and to the neighbor's apartment, where she calls the police from their phone.

Officers arrive and what do you think happens? The obvious response is that David is taken to jail and is to be charged with domestic violence, assault, or some similar charge. Well, you are only half right.

What really happens is that both of them are taken to jail and both charged with assault. Both have to pay a bondsman approximately $300 dollars in order to be released. The idea behind this is that since both parties showed visible signs of injury, then the police arrest both of them.

What is wrong with this picture? *Everything.* This happens not only with people that are in a relationship like the two above, but with just two people who happen to get into a fight because one attacked the other.

Cindy's charges never got filed, and David's did, but how sad and frightening for her that she gets attacked, calls the police for protection, and goes to jail because she fought back and didn't just stand there and let him beat her to death.

I will admit that law enforcement has made great progress in their dealings with domestic violence within the past 25 years. Back in the 1980s, if you were to call the police because your husband was beating you, they would hang up on you and did not respond to these types of calls. I believe it took a number of women dying at the hands of their spouses along with society in general relaxing the outdated notion that wife-beating was something no one talked about and was more or less considered acceptable behavior.

In fact, until around 1902, it was still legal for a man to beat his wife in public as long as the instrument he used to beat her with was no bigger around than his thumb!

Thankfully this attitude has changed and is changing even today towards this type of abuse. Abuse of another human being should not be tolerated in any shape, form or fashion.

Situation 3.

You are driving down the road when you have a blow-out and one of your tires shreds. You pull over, only to discover that there is no jack in the car, so you can't change the tire.

While you are calling everyone you can think of to come help, a car stops. Driving it is a guy named Sam that you used to work with. You never really liked the guy, but he never did anything wrong to you. In fact, right now, you are extremely happy to see him.

He says he will be happy to take you either home or to someone's house that can help you. You agree and get in the car. As you are on your way to your house, he gets pulled over by a patrol officer.

It turns out that he has several traffic tickets that he didn't pay and that have gone into warrants, so he is going to jail. A second officer arrives, and asks you to exit the vehicle. You are explaining to him how you know Sam and about your flat tire. The other officer is searching the vehicle.

All of a sudden you are told to place your hands on the top of the car and are being frisked - patted down from head to toe. You ask what is going on, and the first officer tells you that you are going to jail. You are horrified, and ask why.

He shows you two rather large bundles, one of them being over a pound of marijuana and the other being about two ounces of a white substance. Not knowing what either was, you ask what they are. The cop snidely suggests that you needn't act dumb, but you assure him nervously that you have no idea what either is. He sarcastically informs you that one is marijuana and the other is probably cocaine. He opens the bag, pinches a little out and places it on his tongue. After making a horrible face, he verifies that it is indeed cocaine, as it made his tongue numb.

Shaking by this time, you ask him why you are being taken to jail. After all, you just accepted a ride from Sam, and the car belonged to Sam, and you had never seen either of the packages before.

The second officer informs you as he place handcuffs on your wrists behind your back that under the laws of the State of Texas, the drugs found under the passenger seat, which is where you were sitting, belong to you. The only way to get out of being charged with possession of both would be if Sam claims them as his. Even if he does this, at this time you are going to jail and being charged with felony possession of marijuana and felony possession of cocaine which is a controlled substance. There is a very real possibility that the charges may include intent to distribute, because the amounts are too large to think that either was just for personal use.

You go to jail, and get booked on both charges with the total combined bond amount set at $20,000. It's going to cost you a minimum of $4,000 to get out! We are assuming you get the money from somewhere and get released.

You later find out that Sam had someone come down the next day and pay off his traffic citations and he was out on the street free and clear for a little over $800.

The horrors continue. Your first court date arrives and you show up. You don't have a lawyer, because you only make $9.00 an hour and can't afford one. You tell the district attorney's representative this and fill out an affidavit of inability to pay. However, the judge informs you that since you are gainfully employed that you will have to hire an attorney.

He/she resets your case for three weeks in the future and sternly informs you that you need to have an attorney when you come back the next time and that he/she wouldn't advise showing up without one.

51

Reality is that any attorney, even a bad one, is going to charge you around $5000 to handle your case. Probably over half of this will have to be paid up front before any attorney will take the case. ***You have to come up with the money from somewhere!***

Let's go on ahead in time to the court appearance. Of course, in this scenario, you have somehow come up with the money, most likely borrowing it from a friend or relative. We won't consider the alternative and those possibilities here.

The DA has offered you a "deal" which is deferred adjudication - which I will explain in full very shortly - for a period of 5 years, since this is your first offense. Your lawyer tells you this and you feel like you are living in a nightmare! And indeed you are. The nightmare is called the justice system.

Finally the deal is hammered out to 4 years deferred adjudication and 150 hours of community service. This means you have to volunteer 150 hours of your time to certain selected organizations as a condition of your probation, which is currently referred to as community supervision. These include, but are not limited to, places such as homeless shelters, food banks, and similar places.

All for accepting a ride with someone you were only acquainted with because you had a flat tire. Outrageous! Exactly, but true, true, true. And it happens every day, over and over and over. Once you are arrested and charged with a crime, there is no presumption of innocence. "Innocent until proven guilty." It sounds wonderful, but harsh cold reality is that you are guilty and the only way to stay out of prison is to spend thousands upon thousands of dollars. You are not even treated as if you could possibly be innocent. The jails are full of people who are not guilty of the crimes they have been charged with and convicted of. Just as there are many criminals who perform horrific crimes and never get caught.

This is the perfect opportunity to explain deferred adjudication. This is a type of probation that is served in lieu of a formal conviction. In other words, you are punished for the crime, but if you adhere to all the conditions set forth in the terms, then the indictment (charges) will be dismissed and there will be no conviction. Convicted felons lose many of their rights under the constitution, such as the ability to own and possess a firearm, and to vote. While you are serving out your deferred adjudication, you will not have these rights, but if it is eventually dismissed, your full rights under the Constitution are restored.

You are placed on what is called Community Supervision. You must report to an office and see a "probation" officer – now called a Community Supervision Officer - at least once a month, pay a monthly fee of anywhere from $40 to $100 and submit to drug and alcohol testing in the form of a UA (urinalysis) whenever they so desire. These you also have to pay for and cost less than $20. In theft cases, there may be restitution ordered so that the victim can be paid back for whatever was stolen.

If you fail to do all this, they can revoke your probation (Community Supervision) and convict you of the crime and send you to jail. If they think drugs are part of the problem or the charges were originally for drugs, they can send you to "rehab." Sadly, I have seen this foster dangerous relationships between people who committed worse crimes after they were eventually released. Rehabilitation can and does work, but only when the person *really wants it to.* You can't help a person who doesn't think they need help.

Back to Sam. Let's do the math on your ride with Sam now. $4000 bond, $5000 attorney's fees, four years at $40 per month plus 6 estimated UAs each year at $11 each, and the grand total for your ride home - that never got you there - is $11,184. And for *his* drugs in *his* car and because he had warrants outstanding that gave them probable cause to search the vehicle.

Now that bring us to the biggest lie that is told to everyone who is ever made an offer of deferred adjudication by every attorney and prosecutor and judge in this state and that is this. **If you complete your deferred adjudication and the charges are dismissed, it will not be on your record.**

As I stated, that is the biggest lie ever told and done so by everyone involved and I wish I knew why. It will always be on your record and will never go away – ever!!!

Yes, it is better than a conviction, but it will show up any time someone checks your criminal history for any reason. To be a volunteer at a child's elementary school, in most school districts now, it is necessary to pass a background check. Having a deferred adjudication on your record, even if it is from 10 or 15 years ago will result in being denied and an appeal will have to be filed and approved by the school district before you can eat lunch with the child or attend parties in the classroom. This same procedure will happen each and every year. It doesn't mean you won't be approved, it just means you have to furnish them with the actual dismissal papers from the County Clerk's office, and pay for these by the page, and then they have to discuss you and your criminal history to make a decision to approve you.

Something I find discriminatory involving one particular school district is that when they list the approved volunteers on their website, the names are usually just a person's first and last name. However, those with a criminal history of some kind that do get approved will have their names listed in the same manner as the Department of Public Safety lists the name in their records, usually first name, maiden name, and then married name. In other words, you can pick out the people easily who have smudges in their past and had to be approved by the district's school board.

Attorneys and those in the legal profession will assure you that you can petition the court – of course at a cost of thousands I would assume – for a notice of nondisclosure so that the deferred adjudication will not be reported to those seeking information on your criminal background. The problem with this is that the only agencies that won't be given the information are those that report to the public. That means PublicData.com, USSearch.com or similar places would not be given the information, but school districts, prospective employers, insurance companies, and law enforcement agencies would still be given the information. So what is the use of spending the money?

Another twist in the entire situation is that accepting deferred adjudication requires a person to plead guilty to the crime, so this is construed by many as the fact that you are indeed a criminal. After all, you admitted your guilt.

There is a large company that owns and operates quite a few large apartment communities in the metropolitan area where I live that will not lease an apartment to anyone who has ever been convicted of a felony, filed for bankruptcy, or who has a deferred adjudication on their criminal history.

So in addition to the expenditure of nearly $12,000 for accepting that ride with Sam, you may never be able to lease your own apartment in your own name. This is just one of the probable consequences of this occurrence, and you were guilty of nothing.

That, though ugly, is just a small peek into the realities of our Justice System.

There is nothing "just" about this system. Justice is blind when you see her image, and that was originally intended to be symbolic of the fact that it didn't matter who you were to her, that you were still going to be dealt with equally and fairly. Now I believe it signifies that she has no idea of the atrocities that go on in her halls, and is blind to the fact that the scales rarely balance, unless one side contains mountains of cash.

Let me share with you another experience that I personally witnessed about four years ago in a criminal courtroom in Tarrant County, Texas. A young man was charged with possession of a controlled substance (cocaine) in the amount of less than 1 gram. To refresh you on the metric system, there are a little over 28 grams in an ounce and 16 ounces in a pound. He was sentenced to 5 years Community Supervision deferred adjudication and required to perform 200 hours of Community Service.

The young woman who was next on the docket was charged with possession of a different type of controlled substance (methamphetamine) in the amount of more than 1 ounce (over 56 times more than the young man had) and possession of 2 pounds of marijuana. She was sentenced to 3 years Community Supervision deferred adjudication and *no* Community Service.

Justice should have had a stroke and died at the inequity of just these two cases and the sentences imposed. What I find sad is that this is a daily occurrence. It happens thousands of time daily in hundreds of courtrooms across the state and in all likelihood, all across the country.

I have one last situation to present to you, once again related from an actual experience in the life of a real person in the last few years. This gives you yet another incident in which the justice system failed, and miserably.

Please note that things like this happen every day to people everywhere, and when you see the outcome of this one, you will probably be able to understand why. Please don't let something like this happen to you.

Situation 4.

Brad met Lynn through a mutual friend, and soon they became close friends. Brad was involved in the health/fitness industry, and was one of only two wholesale distributors of a very popular product in the entire state.

One day he and Lynn were talking and he asked her if she would be interested in making some extra money. The plan was to become partners in selling the products at trade shows, of which there were three big ones scheduled in the next month that he was committed to attend. He had some inventory, but due to some problem with his wife's bank, he had no credit card with which to purchase additional items for the upcoming shows.

Lynn agreed that she needed to make some extra money, and they contacted the company, ordered $7500 worth of products, and changed the contact and shipping information in the company's system so that everything would be shipped to Lynn's house in the future. Lynn used her credit card to pay for the merchandise.

The merchandise came and Brad picked it all up. He headed off to the first show, and after is ended, told Lynn they had sold a few items, but as the other show was across the state, he wouldn't be back with all their money until after the next show the coming weekend.

To make a long story short, Lynn never saw Brad, any of the money, nor any of the merchandise she paid for again. Neither did Brad's wife.

Lynn had just been swindled out of $7500.

Now the legal stupidity begins. She calls the police to file theft charges against him, and was told they couldn't help her. Why? Because she *willingly gave him the merchandise,* and there was no written contract. Yes that's right. They told her it was a civil matter.

Now there is some recourse for civil matters. Small claims court handles matters of this nature. But the problem with this avenue is that there is a limit to the amount of any claim that can be presented in this court, and that limit is $5000.

Well, Lynn reasoned, $5000 is better than nothing. Once again, there's a catch. If the amount of the entire thing is more than $5000, you can't proceed. And you can't file two claims in order to recover the entire amount.

So, there was no civil recourse. Lynn decided to contact the District Attorney's office in her county and present the matter to them. She downloaded their complaint form off the internet, filled it out, attached all the required documentation, even including a picture of Brad for easier identification, and returned it to them.

About a month later, she received a letter from their office, stating that from the information provided, they could not find that anything criminal had occurred. They referred her to Small Claims Court. It was obviously a form letter.

Now is that not ridiculous? A licensed attorney telling her to take the matter to a court that they should *know* only handles matters of $5000 or less.

Then to make matters even worse, a couple of months later, there was an article in the newspaper in which a mentally challenged man had been forced to withdraw his 401k from a previous employer who had gone out of business. The money needed to be reinvested somewhere, and his sister helped him handle life situations due to his diminished mental capacities. He told her when she asked about this that he had already invested it, having given the entire amount of over $100,000 to a couple who said they would invest it for him and make him a lot of money. Let me point out that there was no written contract, and he willingly gave them the money. The sister contacted them and was only able after many months to recover some equipment and a car that had been purchased with her brother's retirement fund money, and approximately $6000 cash. She went to the DA's office and they filed criminal charges against the couple. Lynn wrote the DA's office again, sending a copy of the article, pointing out to them the only difference between the two situations was the fact that she wasn't mentally challenged and the amount of money was greater. The rest of the story was basically the same, including the voluntary exchange between two parties of money or merchandise, and the lack of a written agreement.

Can you see much difference in the two other than these two things? Lynn can't and I can't either. However, her last letter has to this date received no reply. Why is something criminal in one instance and not in another? Ask someone in the legal profession. But don't be surprised if they don't have an answer, or one that makes sense.

(As this was being written, a story appeared in the newspaper that unfortunately proved to be a perfect example of something similar to the situation above. I give it to you here. The resolution will be down the road, and the public may never find out what happens. Unfortunately, I think I already know.)

There was a private school that had been operating nearly 40 years. Tuition was $7,000 to $12,000 per child each year. Suddenly, only three weeks before classes were scheduled to begin, the newspaper printed a story telling how the school was closing. Many of the parents found out when they read the newspaper. The sad fact is that all the parents of the 137 children that had registered to attend had already paid the tuition *in advance* for the upcoming school year. One of the members of the school's board of directors was quoted as saying there would be no refunds. Most of the parents had borrowed the money from a credit union, who stated that they will try to extend the notes, or lower the interest rate, but that the loans must be repaid. Yes, there will be many who will try to seek legal avenues to recover their money, and one wonders where the money actually went. There is still a large mortgage on the property, but the story didn't mention any past-due amounts or impending foreclosures, so where did $1,000,000 or more go and what did it pay for?

Do you think the parents will get any of it back? I seriously doubt it. Will they be able to go to court to recover any of it? I doubt it. Remember, small claims court has a limit of $5000, and they willingly gave the school their money, so there is probably no recourse. They may have even had written contracts that are now meaningless. Lynn can sympathize with all of you, and there are many many others.

Therefore, please be aware that in my opinion, there is no such thing as justice and the system is all about money and who can pay their attorney the most. Be aware that there is also no presumption of innocence, and when you think you have some legal rights as the victim of a crime, you probably don't and may even be seen as the criminal.

In closing, let me make you aware of one more ridiculous aspect of the law in my state. If a 17-year-old gets arrested for anything, they are automatically tried as an adult. In order to hire an attorney, a person must sign a contract for services. But a 17-year-old can't enter into a legal contract because they are not an adult. To legally contract for anything, a person must be 18 years old. So the kid can go to prison for a crime, but can't legally hire his own attorney to represent him. Is that not stupid?

I think it is, as are so many things in our so-call justice system.

In case you want to read about any of the laws and legal issues I have mentioned in this chapter, you can refer to the Texas Statutes. The Code of Criminal Procedure and the Government Code are treasure troves of information about all kinds of things, especially the type of things I have discussed here. If you happen to be enrolled in a Criminal Justice class, your teacher can direct you to them if you aren't already familiar with them. Our legislature has a great website where information such as this can be found. And if you live in another state, your statutes and laws are also available, probably online, but if not, the Reference section of your local library is a great place to start.

Once again, my goal is to make you aware of things that really happen in this world, and though not fair (the little voice should be hoarse by now after this last chapter!), they *are* the way they are, and are not likely to change anytime soon.

You need to realize that one little mistake, maybe not even your own, may end up costing you the rest of your life. Everyone makes mistakes, but if that mistake gets you entangled in the legal system, then not only will it cost you or your parents enough money to buy you a car, but it could and will shadow you the rest of your life. It is no fun to feel like a criminal, but that is what you will feel like every time someone runs a background check on you. And even though "they" always say that even a conviction may not prevent you from getting whatever it is you are applying for, you have to be realistic enough to know that they will favor the person with a spotless record over and above the one with even the smallest smudge. Even if it was many years in the past. It is still there and always will be and don't believe anyone who tells you any different. They are lying to you, and I really believe that most of them know they are lying to you. But they all stick together and all of them tell the same lie.

The wheels of justice turn extremely slowly, and as far as I'm concerned aren't headed anywhere but to the bank to make a large deposit.

One Last Word

Here is one final real-life example like the others I have given you to teach you that everything you do not only affects you but others as well. And in this instance, it might affect you in ways you would never want.

Apparently, some young adults/teenagers have decided it is "fun" to text naughty/nude pictures of themselves or others to their friends. This stupidity is called "sexting". And yes, I called it stupid. And it is very stupid.

Why? Very simple. It is a crime to possess, publish, or knowingly partake in the production and/or distribution of pornographic pictures of a child. Anyone under the age of 18 is considered a child. Therefore, that naked picture you take of yourself to send to your friend could land both of you in prison on child pornography charges. And these are prosecuted very aggressively, as this is one of the most horrible crimes committed in this country (or anywhere in the world) and one for which punishments are extremely stiff. And in addition, those found guilty of this may have to register everywhere they ever live as a sex offender. For the rest of their life.

Quite a price to pay for one picture, now isn't it? Could it possibly happen to you? You bet it could. Don't go through life believing that you are "immune" from the things that affect "other people". You are one of the group and there is no immunity!

Live your life SMART, not oblivious to truth. You will go a lot further.

Final Thoughts

Well, you have finished it. I hope you have enjoyed it.

If I succeeded in putting many questions in your head that weren't already there, then I am happy. If I succeeded in making you angry at times, then I am happy.

This book could have been much longer and much more detailed. However, for my intended audience, that would have been a "death sentence" for its message. I would have lost your attention and your ability to understand.

The longest journey begins with a single step. Your life is a journey. Whatever you decide to do with it, and any direction that it takes, the journey has already begun. However, there will be changes in direction, and those smaller journeys within the life journey sometimes can be frightening. Take that first step and you have begun that journey. Do it with joy and positive expectations and you can't lose.

I wish to close and leave you with a quote from Ralph Waldo Emerson that I find inspiring. So much so that I have it framed and hanging on the wall beside my computer. This quotation is about *success*.

"To laugh often and much
To win the respect
Of intelligent people
And the affection of children;
To earn the appreciation
Of honest critics and endure
The betrayal of false friends;
To appreciate beauty,
To find the best in others;
To leave the world
A bit better, whether
By a healthy child,
A garden patch
Or a redeemed social condition;
To know even one life
Has breathed easier
Because you have lived.
That is to have succeeded."